I0161024

Lyrics From My Soul

Sobreta Lady Breezee Harris

Volume 1

Copyright © 2016 by **Sobreta Lady Breezee Harris**

All rights reserved. No part of this publication may be reproduced, distributed or transmitted in any form or by any means, without prior written permission.

Sobreta Lady Breezee Harris
ladybreezee@yahoo.com
www.ladybreezee.com

Publisher's Note: This is a work of fiction. Names, characters, places, and incidents are a product of the author's imagination. Locales and public names are sometimes used for atmospheric purposes. Any resemblance to actual people, living or dead, or to businesses, companies, events, institutions, or locales is completely coincidental.

Book Layout © 2017 BookDesignTemplates.com

Cover Design by Yvette Cage

Author Photo by Jarrid Harris – Clear Media Group

Lyrics From My Soul/ Sobreta Lady Breezee Harris. -- 1st ed.
ISBN 978-0-692-69034-5

DEDICATION

This book is dedicated to my mother, Naomi Katie Scott Junius! She transitioned many years ago but is still a very real and vital part of my life! She strengthens me even today, in more ways than one.

ACKNOWLEDGEMENTS

I thank my Heavenly Father for giving me the gift of poetry and the Holy Spirit for speaking the lyrics into my soul. I thank my husband, Alan Wayne Harris, Sr., for loving and supporting me; the hugs and the "you did good baby" comments. Thank you for giving me the name, Lady Breezee, as I am called when I perform my poetry! Thank you for those moments you've given me the space and time I needed to write and memorize. Love you so much babe! Thank you to each person (you know who you are) who ever spoke into my life, pushed me, prophesied to me, encouraged me and complimented me regarding my poetry and my first book. To those I've performed with on stage, thank you for your support and motivation. To my favorite artist and sister-friend since the 10th grade, Yvette Cage, I love you so much! Thank you for this awesome book cover. I pray this book blesses the lives of all who read it.

May you experience peacefulness where no turmoil or chaos can find!

~ LADY BREEZEE

Table of Contents

What Is Poetry For Me?

What is poetry for me
It's a method of expressions
It's a vehicle for confessions
It's a way of sharing visions
And making impressions
It's never been about a competition for me
I write because it frees you and it frees me
For me, it's all about ministry
God gives me messages to deliver lyrically
Therefore I'd rather be a blessing to the hearers
And allow them to see Jesus in me
So, I write the lines
From my heart
And I speak the lyrics
To impart
To reach the hearts and minds of others
Of my sisters and my brothers
In Christ
And those not yet in Christ
So, you see
I write with a mission
Because God has given me a commission
To compel mankind to come
And be joint heirs with Christ
And become one
With Him
If I can change a heart or a mind
With what I write
Then I have accomplished what God has assigned
And that's not all I write about though
I write about love and joy
Sadness and gladness
To give others hope
To let them know that no matter what

They can cope
I want people to feel God's touch
And know that He loves them so much
So, I write from my heart
The Holy Spirit as my counterpart
I love poetry
It's all in me
I feel the lyrics on the inside of me
When it doesn't make you run and shout
It still gives you something to think about
I write what God leads me to write about
What is poetry for me?
It's about helping the hearers and the readers be free
And change mentally
Lyrically speaking by Lady Breezee

My Story

Let's talk about low self-esteem
Now don't get it twisted
I'm not asking for pity
Just sharing my story
When I was a kid, I didn't think I was pretty

A lot of the kids teased me
Because one of my eyes were crossed
After I was born I had to have surgery
To correct both, the left and the right
The left eye yielded to the procedure
But the right eye enjoyed its crooked sight

I don't know how a crossed eye equates to ugly
But that's what the other kids thought
A few of them even called me fugly
And honey, their lies I bought

I didn't understand why older people
Called me beautiful
And the younger kids didn't think the same way
You see when I looked in the mirror
I always saw a pretty face on display

Yet the more I heard the derogative
The more I tended to believe the negative
And greater feelings of not being good enough

And I felt that, in some crowds, I was inadequate
And I didn't belong

No one really knew or cared
How I felt on the inside
I just kept my feelings to myself
I was embarrassed about my feelings
My lack of self-worth and pride

Every now and then
Someone would see right through me
I can tell that person really cared
And would try their best to encourage me
To help me see my true identity

It wasn't until my early twenties
That I was delivered from low self-esteem
God taught me how to truly love myself
And accept that I was created to be
Better than what it seemed

I walk in freedom today
Because I know who I am in Christ
I am fearfully and wonderfully made
Beautiful on the inside and out
For my life He ultimately sacrificed

Breaking Free

Breaking free
Of what I claimed to be
Finally recognizing
Who and what
I was meant to be

Made attempts to change
How I interacted
Just so I can fit in
With the so-called in crowd
Not the normal way I acted

Maturity and growth set in
Soon enough
Made me realize that
I am a loving person
Who didn't have to pretend to be tough

I finally got the revelation
That some people really did love me for me
Had to stop believing the lies I was told
I had to learn to love me freely

No more chains holding me
You see
Because I have been completely set free
To love me for who I was created to be
No one else but me

Don't Give Up

Just when you were about to give in
God showed His love and stepped in
Just when you were about to give up
God, in all His power, showed up
When you thought you danced your last dance
You decided to give God another chance
Instead of taking it upon yourself to fight
Allow God's Word to give you greater insight
God is the same yesterday, today and forevermore
He has your back now just like He did before
No matter what others do
Don't give up on Him
Remember He will fill your cup
And fill it to the brim
No matter what life looks like today
Don't give up on God and please continue to pray
He loves you today
Just like He did that day
When you asked Him to come into your heart
He promised you from the start
That His love for you will never part
So continue to stand on His Word
And cry out to Him
Trust me, your voice will still be heard

Trust In The Lord

Trust in the Lord with all thine heart
And lean not to thine own understanding
This is not a cliché or an old wives' tale
Notwithstanding (nevertheless, in spite of) what you may be
going through
He wants you to lean on Him
And keep standing
On His Word

Even in times of misunderstanding
The Word of God declares in all thy getting
Get an understanding

When your prayers to God are a tone of demanding
He just may remind you of His Word of commanding
That you acknowledge Him in all your ways

When you don't
Then you find yourself in a place of
Misunderstanding His will and His way

When you seek Him wholeheartedly
You will find that your faith will rise
And that your faith will begin expanding
Then when other trials come
Your faith is now withstanding
You will know God's got you

And that your faith in Him has been longstanding
Because you now trust in Him and acknowledge Him as being
downright upstanding
We may never understand why He does what He does
Or why He allows what He allows
But we know that our God is absolutely and awesomely
Outstanding
So please put your faith, trust, hope and understanding
In Him

What's impossible to us is possible to God
Stop allowing your faith to experience crash-landing
Be strong in the Lord and in the power of His might
Notwithstanding
The tricks the enemy throws your way

We are boldly standing
And declaring
That God has given us power over the enemy

So, grab a hold of God's peace that surpasses all understanding
And keep standing
Standing
On the Word of God

Conversation in the Spirit Realm

Who am I? Where do I belong?
I find myself asking and wondering
Why am I so weak? Why am I not strong?
And yet I keep hearing, "Baby just hold on!"

What is my purpose? What am I to do?
Why am I sometimes unhappy and so very sad?
Some of my days are filled with melancholy
And I feel so blue
And yet something inside tells me I must hold on to You!

Have I gone so far away that I cannot be reached?
Seems that no one is around to help carry my burden
Or is it just that I'm not living out the message that I've preached?
Hold on, I hear, this contract I have with you will never be breached!

Lord have I strayed that far away from you?
That I can't hear You, feel You, see You?
What have I done that's so wrong?
Sometimes I feel like a falling star
Lost and can't find my way.
Then I hear, "You can never go too far! Continue to hold on and you'll see My love is here to stay!"
If you can't hear Me, it's because you're not listening
If you pay attention, you'll see My love is forever glistening
You'll see that everywhere you turn I'm there
You must believe and know that I love you and I care"

So, Lord, are You saying to me
That my eyes need to be open to You
So that I can have the spiritual ability

To see that You love and care for me?

So, as long as I put my faith and trust in You
I can handle whatever life brings my way
And as long as I keep my hands in Your hands
And feast on your Word
I can make it from day to day?

Lord, as long as, I have You
I can carry on through the hardships of life
You've given me the will to push past
Any and all struggles and strife

I now have the cure
God plus prayer will help me to endure

He Protects Me

He protects me and He keeps me
I know beyond a shadow of a doubt
He will never leave me

He is God over my problems
He is God over my pain
He is God over any mountain that I face
He's my sunshine, He's my rain

God is bigger than the problems I've created
He allows me to make mistakes
And see the error of my ways
He makes me aware of the steps I must take
To avoid the enemy's traps and delays

He protects me and He keeps me
He constantly reminds me that I am His
He's everywhere that I am
He's not super mysterious, He just IS

He's the great I Am that I Am
And that's all I need to know
I trust in Him
And He leads me where I need to go

As long as I'm with Him
I have no worries or fears
He assures me that He's concerned about me
And He's the tissue for my tears

He protects me and He keeps me
He loves me like no other can
I'm the apple of His eyes
I've been in His perfect plan
Since this world began

The Holy Spirit

The Holy Spirit gives us power
　　He's with us every single hour

He guides us throughout the day
　　He leads us along the way

He teaches us in the way we should go
　　He tells us what we need to know

The Holy Spirit gives us direction
　　He gives us daily protection

Let Him take control of you
　　Trust Him, He knows what to do

He will be your guiding light
　　He will make your pathway bright

He'll give you a new tongue to pray
　　He'll even tell you what to say

The Holy Spirit, He is the way
　　Invite Him to fill you today!

Purify Me

Lord, I want to be made whole
Lord, I want to be made new
Lord, I need you to fill me through and through

Lord, I desire to be who You need me to be
Lord, I desire to be the one who You've called me to be
Lord, I need you to fill me over and over again

Purify me Oh God! Purify me!
Purify me Oh God for Your Glory!

Lord, I need You to cleanse my heart
Lord, I need You to make me white as snow
Lord, I need You to cover me with Your precious blood

Lord, I want Your peace to fill me
Lord, I need Your joy to overtake me
Lord, I need You to saturate me with Your anointing

Purify me Oh God! Purify me!
Purify me Oh God for Your Glory!

Purify me to do Your Will, Oh God
Purify me to walk in the path You have chosen for me
Purify me to destroy yokes of bondage
Purify me to break the chains that are binding

Relationship with God

My relationship with God is like no other
It's stronger than a relationship with a sister or a brother
He's always there for me and I can depend on Him
I can always call on Him morning noon or night
He never screens my calls
His love for me flows heavier than Niagara Falls
He tells me when I'm right
He corrects me when I'm wrong
He builds me up when I'm down
And He gives me strength to make me strong
I can call on Him when I'm feeling low
Whenever I'm sad and depressed you will never know
Because He causes my face to display a joyful glow
There's no way I'd ever trade my relationship with Him
He will never leave me stuck out on a limb
When I need a friend, He's always there
No one could tell me that my God doesn't care
This is one relationship that I could never trade
And when I fall into His arms, I feel His love will never fade
Don't misunderstand
This love is definitely reciprocated
I freely love God with all my heart
And I didn't have to be manipulated
How much He loves me was revealed
His love makes my heart skip a beat
It would be a sin to keep this relationship concealed
This love relationship is not up for negotiation
Not at all since Jesus is my propitiation
And for that I humbly thank Him
Oh, how dare I forget

The wonderful relationships He's blessed me with
Each one of my children
And my honey, the love of my life
God did a great thing when He made me His wife
Yes, I came to boast
I must testify of this love relationship
From coast to coast
My God is truly the utmost

That's Love

There's no other love like God's love
He loves us and calls us His own
He loves us when we're living right
He loves us when we're living wrong
Because God loves us so much
It should cause us to love our sisters and our brothers
No matter what challenges or problems we face
We must witness and spread His love to so many others
Jesus teaches us what love really is and shows us a more
excellent way
Paul penned it to the Church of Corinth back in the day
Love is patient and love is kind
Love causes hate to go blind
Love swallows all manner of envious
And crushes the evil that attempts to make us devious
Love does not boast and is not full of pride
In our hearts and our lives God's love must abide
Love bears all things
Love doesn't run out the back door when problems and
issues knock on the front door
Love believes all things
Love trusts God and stands on His Word
Love hopes all things.
Love has faith in God and seeks Him for everything
Love will stand through it all
Love knows that trouble lasts only for a little while
and will pick you up when you fall
Love loves through the thick and the thin.
Love says we are victorious
We always win

Love rather understands
Than dish out harsh commands
And demands confusion to take a back seat
Love withstands tests and trials and overcomes defeat
Love prepares the way for us to be forgiving
Which is a true example of Godly living
Love, God's love, should be a part of our everyday lives
This is the great commandment for which the Christian
always thrives
Love those who you often see
The ones you say are hard to love
And learn to love them unconditionally
So that you can be free
To love

I Was Not Built to Break

Luke 10:19 tells me
That God has given me the authority
To tread on serpents and scorpions
He has given me power over all the power of the enemy
And assures me that nothing,
By any means, will hurt me
According to this, I am confident
That I was not built to break
No matter what storms in my life may quake
So, when I'm faced with situations
That seem too difficult or hard
All I need to do is stand on God's Word
And depend on the Holy Spirit
For He is my spiritual body guard
See, God created me to stand
Against the tricks of the enemy
He taught me how to understand
How the enemy operates
I've learned not to even entertain
The enemy and his conglomerates
Because God won't put more on me than I can take
To God be the Glory
I was not built to break
Trials and tribulations come and go
And at times it seems as though we may not make it
But the way God has shown up
Time and time again
There's now no doubt in my mind
Baby, I know that I can take it
I'm not standing before you as a fake

Remember, I told you
I was not built to break
God has caused me to have much faith in Him
He has never yet let me down
Isaiah reminds me to not fear
When the waters of life begin to rise
My God will not allow me to drown
My brothers and my sisters
I was not built to break
Even when I've asked the question,
Lord, how much more can I take?
He reminds me that
The joy of the Lord is my strength
He is strong in times when I am weak
So when I need encouragement
It is God's face that I seek
When my body is in pain
And during times when in my heart
There's an ache
The Holy Spirit is there to remind me
I was not built to break
And I will end with this
When my faith is tempted
And all hell breaks loose and causes my faith to shake
The Spirit of the Lord lifts up a standard
And I proudly proclaim
I was not built to break

Divine Protection

I'm protected Divinely
You can't block me
You can't stop me
Because I'm protected Divinely
By God above
You cannot deceive me
You cannot police me
I'm protected Divinely
By Jesus' precious blood
You may try to bind me
And hold me down
You may even try to blind me
But you'd be wasting your time
The God I serve causes the blind to see
So please believe me
When I tell you
I'm protected Divinely
I walk in much faith you see
I trust in the God who parted the Red Sea
He has my back consistently
Because my steps are ordered by Him
I can stomp on the ugly head of the enemy
By now you should know
I'm protected Divinely
The blood of Jesus covers me
God's mighty Hand is upon me
Therefore, the enemy has no power over me
I have no fear because God is with me
He will not allow the waters to overtake me

And no fire that I may go through can consume me
His Word assures me
That He will never leave me
And He lives on the inside of me
His Holy Spirit leads and guides me
When darkness is all around me
He lightens my path so that I can still see
His will and His purpose for me
I'm not hiding from the enemy
In fear of what he can do to me
God says in His Word
Do not fear those who can kill the body but not the soul
But fear the one who can kill both body and soul
And cast into hell for all eternity
I'm protected divinely
You cannot prevent me
From serving the God who sent me
And you surely can't tempt me
Through deception and foolery
For God has already made a way of escape for me
God grants me abundant grace daily
And He loves me unconditionally
And for that, I walk with my head held high proudly
Why?
Because I'm protected
Divinely

Mind Right

Clutter, clutter, clutter in my mind
Trying to stay focused
Too many distractions of every kind

I have to get my focus where it belongs
When I try, my mind seems to wander to thoughts that are wrong

I need to clear my mind
I need to think straight
I need to begin to focus on things of God small and great

I need to keep my mind "Stayed on Jesus" as the old folks say
But, how do I do that?
Meditate, that's it, Meditate
Meditate on God's Word

You see, when my thoughts begin to line up with God's Word
Foolishness and all ungodly distractions can no longer be heard

I've got to get my mind right
I've got begin to use my God-given insight
I've got to begin to study His Word
So that the Word can take root
Then, I can give the devil the boot

I've got to keep my mind stayed on Jesus
That would keep me from thinking the wrong things
I've got to keep my mind stayed on Jesus
It would help me learn how to deal with the struggles life brings

Sometimes I'm just so tired
Sometimes I'm just too weak
But if I keep my mind stayed on Jesus,
I will no longer live in defeat

You see, I'm not perfect
Not by a long shot
But I've come to realize that Jesus is all I got

I know that if I keep my mind stayed on Jesus
I will definitely get better
I've got to get in that Word and get it together

I need to free my mind and let it be clear
So I can heed God's Word when He speaks in my ear

I've got to get my mind right
I've got to use my God-given insight
I want God to be pleased with me
I want Him to set my mind free

This is not just for me
This not just a mere poem or beautiful poetry
This is for you, you and you
So you too can be free

So, how about you?
Do you desire to do what God has for you to do?
Come on soldier, get your mind right
You can't get into heaven if all you want to do is steal, cheat and
fight

Be obedient to God's Word
So your prayers will not go unheard

So come on and follow Lady Breezee
I'm not saying this walk will be easy
But it will sure keep you from a life of hell and burning eternally

Get your mind right!!

You Are My God

Hide me in Your secret place
Where safety is
You are my strength

Wrap me in Your loving arms
Where protection is
You are my peace

Speak softly to my soul
Where comfort is
You are my joy

Lead me in the way I should go
Where direction is
You are my guide

Direct my path as I lean on You
Where trust is
You are my God

Who Is God To You

Hello God, It's me again
I'm testifying of how
You brought me through thick and thin
You kept me when I didn't know
How the story would end
Then there were times I couldn't hear Your voice
And thought You had forgotten about me
And I forgot all about my testimony
I became angry because I didn't think
You were still there
I really didn't realize You still care
So, I decided to pray and spend more time in Your Word
You became more real to me after what I read and my spirit
heard
So many people doubt You
And don't know anything about You
I desire to see those people set free
So they too can have a powerful testimony
I just wonder sometimes when I look in the faces of Your
people and want to ask them,
'Who is God to you?'
God has brought me through some tough times in my life
He has seen me through a lot of pain, misery and strife
He keeps a smile on my face
And has given me so much grace
God has always been there for me
And He has truly seen me through
But I ask of you curiously
And please be true
'Who is God to you?'

When you awake each morning
To a brand, new dawning
Who do you give the credit to?
To whom is your thanks and praise due
For giving you the gift of today
And allowing you to see another day
And starting you on your way?
Whether you know it or not
God has really been good to you
There is so much that God has done
First by sending His only begotten Son
To save our souls from sin
And shown us that with Him we win
I'm sure you can count the times
And pennies, nickels and dimes
When God has reached out His hand
To pull you out of the quicksand
So, again, I ask you
And please be true
Who is God to you?

WORSHIP POEM

It's me God
Coming to You the only way I know how
In pure and true worship
So please Lord hear me now
I worship You, oh God, for who You are
I worship You, oh God
Because You are my shining star
You guide my path and light my way
You keep me from going astray
And although there are times when You seem so far
I know you hear me and I know You care
I know no matter where I am
You will always be there
So I worship You even from afar
You pulled out of a miry muck
You pulled me from places where I was jammed and stuck
When I thought there was no way out
I worship you because You always give me something
To testify about
Even in those times it seemed my heart was made of steel
You proved to me time and time again
That Your love for me is real
So I worship You for who You are
I worship You because there is none like You
You're awesome in power and might
You're Holy and greater than all that is right
You are just and You are divine
I am Yours and You are mine
Sometimes I'm so caught up in You
That I can't form the words to describe You

Can't even think of how to say....
But my love for You is forever on display
There is none like You
You are Creator of all mankind
You made the lame to walk and healed the blind
My God, You are truly One of a kind
Those are just a few reasons why I worship You
You are worthy to be worshipped
There is none like You
And I will continue to worship You
Until there's nothing else left to do

Unbelief

Lord, help my unbelief
Beyond my faith I cannot see
For all the things done by the adversary
Lord, help me to believe with all my heart
I can't tell where the good times and bad times part
It's hard to believe in this world today
Sometimes it's harder to pray
Some say
Money is funny, change is strange
No cents in my pocket
No sense to call on His Name
And you say in Your Word to believe
Lord, help my unbelief
The rent is due and the bills are too
Car note is late and no food to put on my plate
And You say in Your Word to believe
Lord, help my unbelief
Body racking with pain full of hate and shame
No place to call home and I'm just so all alone
And it's written in Your Word to only believe
Lord, help my unbelief
Now I did read somewhere in Your Word
That You give us power to get wealth
And Paul prayed that we would be in health
Then You said if we pay the tenth
That we won't have to worry about one red sent
Because You will rebuke the devour for our sake
And that a way of escape for us You will make
It's written in Psalms to not put your trust in man
Yeah I know, man will leave You sinking in the sand
I hear the song say trust in the Lord and never doubt
For He will surely bring you out
Now I remember when I read in Your Word where you said
I will receive what I ask and believe if I prayed

I prayed when I was hungry and a knock came at the door
No one was there but bags of food were on the floor
I prayed when I was sick and You healed my body quick
I prayed when I was all alone and then an encouraging word
came through the phone
Now that I look back I can recall every reason to believe
Because of that I know that there's nothing I cannot achieve
Forgive me Lord for my unbelief
Faith is the substance of things I hope for
The evidence of what I can't see
I now believe Lord that what I'm praying for, You will give to me
Lord I believe that I'm no longer broke but I'm wealthy
Lord I believe that I'm no longer sick but I'm healthy
Lord I believe that whenever I'm unable, You will help me
I believe Your Word is true
I believe You can and will do what You say You will do
I believe in You and who You are
I believe You are the bright and morning Star
I believe You are the Alpha and Omega
The beginning and the end
I believe You are my only true and trusted friend
I believe You will wipe my every tear away
And I believe Your love is here to stay
I believe that with faith and hope and trust
That Your presence is forever with us
You are my provider and my guide
You are the only way, I know, I've tried
Lord I thank You for helping my unbelief
You are THEE One, my savior, my relief

Peace

That tranquil place where calmness dwells
Where silence envelopes all thoughts
And from the serene surroundings the heart swells
As mindless thoughts bring uninhibited pleasure
The troubles of the day stand still
For the joys that spring forth, there is no measure
Basking in the harmony of the wind as it freely blows
The nostrils inhale nature's healthy aroma
And peaceful plethora of nothingness flows
Where there is no need for understanding
Where reason doesn't matter
Where solace is expanding
And grief and disappointment are disbanding Lying still and
enjoying the meadows of cheerfulness
No worries
No cares
No fears
No tears
No interruptions
No disruptions
No eruptions
Of yelling, of disagreements, of uneasiness, of conflicts, of
displeasures
Where there's a sigh of relief, of quietness, of love for God, of
love for self, of love for health, of love for wealth
Where all the heart's treasures abide
Peace, that sweet comfortable heavenly domain
A realm that's beyond any and all comprehension
A place where bliss, placidity and relaxation reign
May the peace of God consume your heart and your mind
And take you to places so divine, that only He can
May you experience peacefulness where no chaos
Or turmoil can find! Peace!

About the Author

Sobreta Lady Breezee Harris is a wife and mother in a wonderfully blended family of 6 adult, gifted, creative and talented children (Candance Winfield Brown, Jonathan and Jared Winfield; Alan, Jr., Jarrid and Brandon Harris). She's a licensed minister called to evangelism, a poet, a motivator, an encourager, a worship leader and songwriter. Sobreta is originally from New Orleans, LA and currently resides in Houston, TX with her family. She has been writing poetry for as long as she can remember. She's been delivering her poetry as a Spoken Word Artist since 2008. Sobreta is a graduate of Southern University at New Orleans where one of her favorite subjects was Creative Writing.

www.ingramcontent.com/pod-product-compliance
Lightning Source LLC
Chambersburg PA
CBHW060558100426
42742CB00013B/2608